PRAYERS FROM THE ARK
and
THE CREATURES' CHOIR

Rumer Godden was born in England in 1907 but spent much of her childhood in India. She has since lived alternately in both countries and at one time remarked that she was "always a little homesick for one country or the other." India is often the setting of her novels, which have been universally praised for their delicate prose, subtle psychology, and spellbinding atmosphere. They include *Black Narcissus*, *The River*, *A Candle for St. Jude*, and *An Episode of Sparrows*. Her most recent novel is *The Peacock Spring*, a story of two English girls in an India that few Westerners ever see.

The life of Carmen Bernos de Gasztold is recounted by Miss Godden in the epilogue following *The Creatures' Choir*.

Prayers

and

Illustrations by
JEAN PRIMROSE

FROM THE *Ark*

THE *Creatures' Choir*

by
CARMEN BERNOS DE GASZTOLD

*Translated from the French
and with Forewords and an Epilogue by*
RUMER GODDEN

PENGUIN BOOKS

PENGUIN BOOKS
Published by the Penguin Group
Penguin Books USA Inc.,
375 Hudson Street, New York, New York 10014, U.S.A.
Penguin Books Ltd, 27 Wrights Lane, London W8 5TZ, England
Penguin Books Australia Ltd, Ringwood, Victoria, Australia
Penguin Books Canada Ltd, 10 Alcorn Avenue,
Toronto, Ontario, Canada M4V 3B2
Penguin Books (N.Z.) Ltd, 182–190 Wairau Road, Auckland 10, New Zealand

Penguin Books Ltd, Registered Offices:
Harmondsworth, Middlesex, England

Prayers from the Ark

First published in France under the titles:
Le Mieux Aime and *Prières dans l'Arche*
Copyright 1947, 1955, by Editions du Cloître,
Limon par Igny, Seine et Oise
Viking Compass Edition published 1969
Reprinted 1970, 1971, 1973, 1974

The Creatures' Choir

First published in France under the title:
Choral de Bêtes
Copyright © Editions du Cloître, Limon par Igny,
Seine et Oise, 1960, 1965
Viking Compass Edition published 1970
Reprinted 1971, 1973

Published in a one-volume edition in Penguin Books 1976

15   17   19   20   18   16

English text Copyright © Rumer Godden, 1962, 1965
All rights reserved

ISBN 0 14 058.677 6

Library of Congress catalog card number: 76-8041

Printed in the United States of America
Set in Monotype Bembo

Some of these poems first appeared in *McCall's*.

CONTENTS

Prayers from the Ark, which now includes the poems of a smaller book, *Le Mieux Aimé,* has had what could be called a hidden life, being published by the Éditions du Cloître, the private press of the Benedictine Abbaye Saint Louis du Temple at Limon-par-Igny, France, where the poet lives and works. Though they have gone through none of the normal commercial channels, they have sold over thirty thousand copies in France and, in a German version, are selling equally well in Germany and Austria.

I came upon them by accident and was instantly caught by their charm, but do not be alarmed; the charm has nothing to do with whimsy: Carmen de Gasztold has seen too much of the seamy side of life to be a sentimental animal lover—ironically, she has little use for pets. In her world a dog is to guard the house, a horse to work its strength out for its master, a pig to be eaten, and there is an economy and sense about her work that is typically French; it is the truthfulness of the prayers, especially as it re-reflects on us, unthinking humans, that causes pain.

When I resolved to try to translate them it was almost a detective work, both in London and Paris, to find the poet; even when I had traced her to the Abbaye in its wide, rolling green park, it took time to win her confidence and that of her nun advisers—a novelist does not, one might agree, seem a proper person to translate a poet. Nor were these easy poems; their very simplicity makes them difficult. The economy of words, the subtle play on the double meaning of some of them, the integral rhythm, have been almost impossible to catch, and there is in each some phrase or word that is utterly elusive.

How, for instance, in "The Lark," can one render in English the opening,

> *Me voici, ô mon Dieu,*
> *Me voici, me voici!*

with the insistent, shrilling sound of that French i-i-i? Or find a word, in "The Little Bird," for *intarissable*—"*cette intarissable musique*" that repeats the sound and meaning? All our corresponding words seem to be weighted with "sh." Or in "The Old Horse" replace that word *encense* in

> *Ma pauvre tête encense*
> *toute la solitude de mon coeur!*

which gives, in two syllables, the double picture of the old horse's swinging head and a censer swinging to "offer up" in the Catholic sense all that he has left, his loneliness? The dictionary translation of *encenser*, which, when used of a horse, means "to toss," is too young and gay.

I am unhappily aware that I have not come anywhere near the poems' original worth. Perhaps a better poet could have found better answers; I do not know. But I do know that I have seldom had more rewarding hours than those spent working over these poems, first at Stanbrook Abbey, here in England, then with Carmen Bernos de Gasztold herself in the Abbaye parlour, helped from behind the grille by the two nuns in charge of the Éditions du Cloître.

These poems are prayers, Catholic in origin but catholic also in the sense that they are for everyone, no matter of what creed. Carmen Bernos lives now in an atmosphere of prayer, more importantly of belief, but they have not been influenced by the Abbaye. She is too independent to be influenced by anybody; in fact, she likens herself to her own *Chèvre*, the wild goat, and a goat—besides being wild and free—is obstinate. Most of the prayers were written long before she came to the Abbaye, in a scant hard time in which she had to do uncongenial work in the laboratory of a silk factory near Paris—a time of enemy occupation, hunger, cold, frustration; yet it was then that she was able to find, in each of these workaday, infinitesimal, or unfavoured creatures, not only its intrinsic being but an unexpected grain of incense that wafts it up, consecrates it, and this in the most matter-of-fact way.

The Abbaye has only endorsed what she knew a prayer must be—if it is to have any meaning; not something dreamy or wishful, not a cry to be used in emergency, not even a plea, and not necessarily comforting. A prayer is a giving out, an offering, compounded of honest work and acceptance of the shape in which one has been created—even if it is to be regretted as much as the monkey's—of these humble things added to the great three, faith, hope, and love.

Seigneur,
quelle ménagerie!

ord,
what a menagerie!
Between Your downpour and these animal cries
one cannot hear oneself think!
The days are long,
Lord.
All this water makes my heart sink.
When will the ground cease to rock under my feet?
The days are long.
Master Raven has not come back.
Here is Your dove.
Will she find us a twig of hope?
The days are long,
Lord.
Guide Your Ark to safety,
some zenith of rest,
where we can escape at last
from this brute slavery.
The days are long,
Lord.
Lead me until I reach the shore of Your covenant.

Amen

N'oubliez pas, Seigneur,
que je fais lever le soleil!

Do not forget, Lord,
it is I who make the sun rise.
I am Your servant
but, with the dignity of my calling,
I need some glitter and ostentation.
Noblesse oblige. . . .
All the same,
I am Your servant,
only. . .do not forget, Lord,
I make the sun rise.

Amen

Il n'y a que Vous et moi
pour comprendre
ce que c'est que la fidélité!

Lord,
I keep watch!
If I am not here
who will guard their house?
Watch over their sheep?
Be faithful?
No one but You and I
understands
what faithfulness is.
They call me, "Good dog! Nice dog!"
Words. . .
I take their pats
and the old bones they throw me
and I seem pleased.
They really believe they make me happy.
I take kicks too
when they come my way.
None of that matters.
I keep watch!
Lord,
do not let me die
until, for them,
all danger is driven away.

Amen

. . .protégez de la pluie et du vent
mon petit nid.

Dear God,
I don't know how to pray by myself
very well,
but will You please
protect my little nest from wind and rain?
Put a great deal of dew on the flowers,
many seeds in my way.
Make Your blue very high,
Your branches lissom;
let Your kind light stay late in the sky
and set my heart brimming with such music
that I must sing, sing, sing. . . .
Please, Lord.

Amen

. . .mais une étincelle vivante
dans la douceur de Vos joncs. . .

God,
forever I turn in this hard crystal,
so transparent, yet I can find no way out.
Lord,
deliver me from the cramp of this water
and these terrifying things I see through it.
Put me back in the play of Your torrents,
in Your limpid springs.
Let me no longer be a little goldfish
in its prison of glass,
but a living spark
in the gentleness of Your reeds.

Amen

Pourquoi m'avez-Vous fait si tendre?

Lord,
their politeness makes me laugh!
Yes, I grunt!
Grunt and snuffle!
I grunt because I grunt
and snuffle
because I cannot do anything else!
All the same, I am not going to thank them
for fattening me up to make bacon.
Why did You make me so tender?
What a fate!
Lord,
teach me how to say

Amen

Faites qu'il pleuve demain et toujours.

Dear God,
give us a flood of water.
Let it rain tomorrow and always.
Give us plenty of little slugs
and other luscious things to eat.
Protect all folk who quack
and everyone who knows how to swim.

Amen

Mes sabots sont pleins de gambades. .

God! the grass is so young!
My hooves are full of capers.
Then
why does this terror start up in me?
I race
and my mane catches the wind.
I race
and Your scents beat on my heart.
I race,
falling over my own feet in my joy,
because my eyes are too big
and I am their prisoner:
eyes too quick to seize
on the uneasiness that runs through the whole world.
Dear God,
when the strange night
prowls round the edge of day,
let Yourself be moved by my plaintive whinny;
set a star to watch over me
and hush my fear.

Amen

Me laisserez-Vous sans fin
retomber au creux des sillons,
pauvre oiseau d'argile?

I am here! O my God.
I am here, I am here!
You draw me away from earth,
and I climb to You
in a passion of shrilling,
to the dot in heaven
where, for an instant, You crucify me.
When will You keep me forever?
Must You always let me fall
back to the furrow's dip,
a poor bird of clay?
Oh, at least
let my exultant nothingness
soar to the glory of Your mercy,
in the same hope,
until death.

Amen

Faites que je trouve un beau chardon
et qu'on me laisse le temps de le cueillir.

O God, who made me
to trudge along the road
always,
to carry heavy loads
always,
and to be beaten
always!
Give me great courage and gentleness.
One day let somebody understand me—
that I may no longer want to weep
because I can never say what I mean
and they make fun of me.
Let me find a juicy thistle—
and make them give me time to pick it.
And, Lord, one day, let me find again
my little brother of the Christmas crib.

Amen

Que ma petite parcelle d'ardente vie
se fonde dans la grande activité communautaire. .

Lord,
I am not one to despise Your gifts.
May You be blessed
Who spread the riches of Your sweetness
for my zeal. . . .
Let my small span of ardent life
melt into our great communal task;
to lift up to Your glory
this temple of sweetness,
a citadel of incense,
a holy candle, myriad-celled,
moulded of Your graces
and of my hidden work.

Amen

Ne permettrez-Vous pas, un jour,
que quelqu'un me prenne au sérieux?

Dear God,
why have You made me so ugly?
With this ridiculous face,
grimaces seem asked for!
Shall I always be
the clown of Your creation?
Oh, who will lift this melancholy from my heart?
Could You not, one day,
let someone take me seriously,
Lord?

Amen

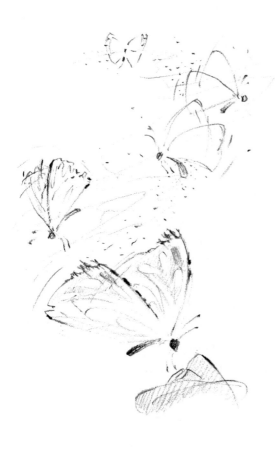

Le vent a peint ses fantaisies
sur mes ailes.

Lord!
Where was I?
Oh yes! This flower, this sun,
thank You! Your world is beautiful!
This scent of roses. . .
Where was I?
A drop of dew
rolls to sparkle in a lily's heart.
I have to go. . .
Where? I do not know!
The wind has painted fancies
on my wings.
Fancies. . .
Where was I?
Oh yes! Lord,
I had something to tell you:

Amen

Je me nourris de choses élevées...

Lord,
I who see the world from above
find it hard to get used to its pettiness.
I have heard it said
You love humble creatures?
Chatter of apes!
It is easier for me
to believe in Your greatness.
I feed on exalted things
and I rather like
to see myself so close to Your heaven.
Humility!
Chatter of apes!

Amen

Seigneur,
je ne suis que poussière et cendre!

Dust and ashes!
Lord,
I am nothing but dust and ashes,
except for these two riding lights
that blink gently in the night,
colour of moons,
and hung on the hook of my beak.
It is not, Lord, that I hate Your light.
I wail because I cannot understand it,
enemy of the creatures of darkness
who pillage Your crops.
My hoo-hoo-hooooo
startles a depth of tears in every heart.
Dear God,
one day,
will it wake Your pity?

Amen

. . .je suis tout petit et très noir. . .

O God,
I am little and very black,
but I thank You
for having shed
Your warm sun
and the quivering of Your golden corn
on my humble life.
Then take—but be forbearing, Lord—
this little impulse of my love:
this note of music
You have set thrilling in my heart.

Amen

Je ne demande rien à personne!

ord,
I am the cat.
It is not, exactly, that I have something to ask of You!
No—
I ask nothing of anyone—
but,
if You have by some chance, in some celestial barn,
a little white mouse,
or a saucer of milk,
I know someone who would relish them.
Wouldn't You like someday
to put a curse on the whole race of dogs?
If so I should say,

Amen

Je suis
comme un petit morceau
de cendre!

Dear God,
would You take Your light
a little farther away
from me?
I am like a morsel
of cinder
and need Your night
for my heart to dare
to flicker out its feeble star:
its hope, to give to other hearts,
what can be stolen from all poverty—
a gleam of joy.

Amen

On ne m'a jamais rien donné.

am so little and grey,
dear God,
how can You keep me in mind?
Always spied upon,
always chased.
Nobody ever gives me anything,
and I nibble meagrely at life.
Why do they reproach me with being a mouse?
Who made me but You?
I only ask to stay hidden.
Give me my hunger's pittance
safe from the claws
of that devil with green eyes.

Amen

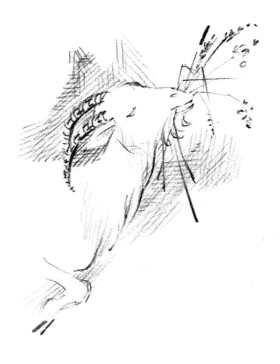

Pour qui seraient Vos montagnes
et ce vent de neige et de sources?

Lord,
let me live as I will!
I need a little wild freedom,
a little giddiness of heart,
the strange taste of unknown flowers.
For whom else are Your mountains?
Your snow wind? These springs?
The sheep do not understand.
They graze and graze,
all of them, and always in the same direction,
and then eternally
chew the cud of their insipid routine.
But I—I love to bound to the heart of all
Your marvels,
leap Your chasms,
and, my mouth stuffed with intoxicating grasses,
quiver with an adventurer's delight
on the summit of the world!

Amen

Je suis bien embarrassé de ma personne...

Dear God,
it is I, the elephant,
Your creature,
who is talking to You.
I am so embarrassed by my great self,
and truly it is not my fault
if I spoil Your jungle a little with my big feet.
Let me be careful and behave wisely,
always keeping my dignity and poise.
Give me such philosophic thoughts
that I can rejoice everywhere I go
in the lovable oddity of things.

Amen

Mon Dieu, donnez-moi du temps.

Dear God, give me time.
Men are always so driven!
Make them understand that I can never hurry.
Give me time to eat.
Give me time to plod.
Give me time to sleep.
Give me time to think.

Amen

Je suis la fable du monde!

Lord,
        I am always made out to be wrong;
        a fable to the whole world.
        Certainly I hoard
        and make provision!
        I have my rights!
        And surely I can take a little joy
        in the fruits of all my work
        without some sob singer
        coming to rob my store?
        There is something in Your justice
        that I scarcely understand,
        and, if You would allow me to advise,
        it might be thought over again.
        I have never been a burden to anybody,
        and, if I may say so,
        I manage my own business very well.
        Then,
        to the incorrigible improvidence
        of some people,
        must I, for all eternity, say

                                        Amen

Un peu de patience,
mon Dieu,
j'arrive!

A little patience,
O God,
I am coming.
One must take nature as she is!
It was not I who made her!
I do not mean to criticize
this house on my back—
it has its points—
but You must admit, Lord,
it is heavy to carry!
Still,
let us hope that this double enclosure,
my shell and my heart,
will never be quite shut to You.

Amen

Je suis Votre serviteur inutile!

See, Lord,
my coat hangs in tatters,
like homespun, old, threadbare.
All that I had of zest,
all my strength,
I have given in hard work
and kept nothing back for myself.
Now
my poor head swings
to offer up all the loneliness of my heart.
Dear God,
stiff on my thickened legs
I stand here before You:
Your unprofitable servant.
Oh! of Your goodness,
give me a gentle death.

Amen

Je ne reviendrai plus dans l'Arche!

I believe,
Lord,
I believe!
It is faith that saves us, You have said it!
I believe the world was made for me,
because as it dies
I thrive on it.
My undertaker's black
is in keeping with my cynical old heart.
Raven land is between You
and that life down there, for whose end I wait
to gratify myself.
"Aha!" I cry. "*Avant moi le déluge!*"
What a feast!
I shall never go back to the Ark!
To the Ark. . .
Oh! let it die in me—
this horrible nostalgia.

Amen

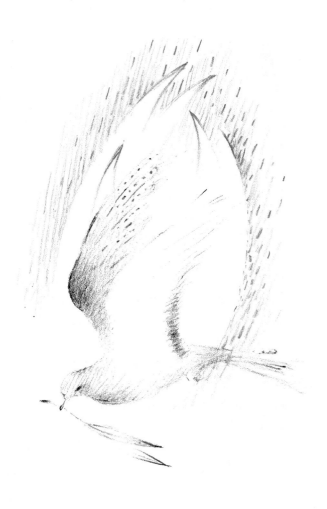

Je suis la simple colombe!

T he Ark waits,
Lord,
the Ark waits on Your will,
and the sign of Your peace.
I am the dove,
simple
as the sweetness that comes from You.
The Ark waits,
Lord;
it has endured.
Let me carry it
a sprig of hope and joy,
and put, at the heart of its forsakenness,
this, in which Your love clothes me,
Grace immaculate.

Amen

Carmen Bernos de Gasztold lives now in the *colombier,* the great dove
house, converted to a guest house, that belongs to the Benedictine
Abbaye of St. Louis du Temple in the rolling French countryside be-
tween Paris and Versailles. The Abbaye, with its farm buildings
and its original château, is walled in its park, but the dove-house tower
stands apart, high and alone in the fields, open to such a wide sweep
of land and sky that it seems the hub of the wheel of creation. From
every window one can watch the landscape: clouds racing across the
sky—this is a windy part of France; the blueness of still days; the larks
winging up from the furrows; the return of the swallows. One can
follow the cycle of the year, the tillage and manuring of the fields,
the sowing and the crops; the seasons of wild flowers and trees; and,
as well, the minuscule shy active life of country creatures. Indeed, that
tower seems a symbol of Carmen de Gasztold's talent in these poems
of *The Creatures' Choir,* in which each creature is itself yet a part of
the large world. "Anyone could write such poems," said one critic
when she first showed them to him. Perhaps the simplest answer to
such obtuseness is that no one but Carmen de Gasztold has ever done it.

Her first book, *Prayers from the Ark,* brought her renown; the in-
itial American printing was sold out in five days; since then there has
been printing after printing: translations into German, Dutch, Spanish,
Finnish, Italian; a recording published by Folkways and exquisitely
spoken in English and French by Marian Seldes, while a setting to
music is on the way. There has been, in fact, a best-selling success,
but *The Creatures' Choir* has not been written as a sequel. I found both

books together some four years ago, when they were in pamphlet form in French, published by the Éditions du Cloître, the Abbaye's private press, in which they had had something of a "hidden life." I resolved then that this second book, too, must be translated.

Most of these new poems are not prayers, in the sense that a prayer is a plea; each animal, bird, fish, reptile, or insect voice makes, as it were, a statement of its situation, its circumstances—what, perhaps, we humans would call its problem. Some of the voices are assertive, lacking the humility that made the Prayers so poignant, but each is exactly true.

I have learned to trust Carmen de Gasztold. Once or twice I questioned a line: "A toad does not *flûte*, as in the French; it croaks." "No," said Carmen, "it sings," and she described for me the toads' night song. Why, I asked myself, does she say of the seagull, that it is a "bird of unending bitterness"—"*l'amertume sans fond*"? On the day I asked that, I found in the London *Times* an account of an old sailor's sea lore in which he said that gulls were possessed of the souls of dead sailormen from Liverpool. "Listen to their cry, 'sca-a-ouse.'" ("Scouse," as every sailor knows, means a Liverpudlian.) Those with black heads, he believed, were once boatswains, black symbolizing the wickedness of their hearts! The English poet Charlotte Mew, too, speaks of Westminster gulls that are old sea captains' souls. Again and again Carmen de Gasztold shows that, in a few lines, she can catch the essence, the *être* of a creature, and without sentimentality—indeed, she discovers that some have most dislikable traits; but why should we take it for granted that beasts are born with "nice" characters? Kindness, the virtue in humanity extolled nowadays more than any other, is completely lacking in animals; yet their faults—if these can be called faults—are redeemed by innocence, a quality human grownups have almost always lost.

Carmen Bernos, as I said in the Preface to *Prayers from the Ark*, lives in an atmosphere of prayer, more importantly of belief, and none of her creatures questions for a moment that it has a creator, but her poems have not been influenced by the Abbaye; she is too independent to be influenced by anyone, and though the poems are Catholic in origin they are catholic also in the sense that they are for everyone, no matter of what creed. In *The Creatures' Choir,* unlike the "Prayers," humans seldom appear; most of the poems are a direct communication between the beast, large or small, and its creator, and the link is as powerful with the flea as with the whale—though the flea, being a flea, is less respectful.

The translation was difficult. The title itself brought a puzzle: the French is *Choral de Bêtes,* but in English "choral" or "chorale" is purely musical and also sounds a little affected, whereas "choir," a company of singers, though not the exact translation, seems to fit the book. The *bêtes:* to those who know of the Queen's Beasts (here in Britain), or of Helen Waddell's beautiful book *Beasts and Saints,* the word has its first meaning, as given in the *Oxford English Dictionary,* of "a living being," which covers animals, birds, fishes, insects, and reptiles. They all have a voice here; but to many who do not have this tradition, "beasts" carries only its meaning of brutishness, coarseness; "creatures," for them, comes nearer to the sense of the original. Thus the book is appearing under different titles: *The Beasts' Choir* in Britain, *The Creatures' Choir* in America.

As always, the smaller the poem, the greater the difficulty of translating, because every word becomes more important, and French to English is perhaps most difficult of all; for instance in what one might dismiss as a trivial matter, the definite article, the French has genders, giving the play on "*le,*" "*la,*" "*les,*" whereas in English there is only "the" that is apt to recur again and again, weighing down a short poem by its thick "th." At times, too, I had to avoid the negative interrogative, which in the English use of the verb "to be" can sound stilted. There are different subtleties of meaning, such as that word "*flûte*" used of the toad: in French it gives the feeling of the range of the instrument's notes, while in England it immediately suggests the treble—and, though the toad sings, it certainly does not sing treble. Again, the rhythms of the two languages are very different: a French gnat has "*la danse de St. Guy*" with its five short dancing syllables, but an English gnat has to suffer from St. Vitus's dance, which sounds slurred and hissing; for the vocation of the French beaver, the poet uses the word "*edifier,*" with its double implication of spiritual raising as well as physical: "to build" is the nearest one can get. These double meanings, the play on words and sounds, run all through the poems. In "The Flea" the word "*puce*" in French means not only a flea but a colour, so that the poet was able to get the double play of "*ma robe puce.*" Translated, the line becomes meaningless, so that we cut it. And there is always the untranslatable phrase such as "*arrière pensée*" in "The Centipede"; "*arrière pensée*" has a suggestion of rancour and darkness, and "afterthought," "second thought" come nowhere near; but "reticences," as Janet Erskine Stuart* said, "expresses thoughts withheld and silences not altogether normal, a little uncanny."

All through the book I was given considerable freedom to transpose lines or "turn" them so as to get what seemed to me not only the best effect but the one closest to the poet's thought.

For us both, it was a time of comradeship: Carmen de Gasztold has no English, but letters and poems, both English and French, went backwards and forwards between the tower in France and my study in England. When I came to the Abbaye itself, we, Carmen and I, were allowed to work in one of the parlours with the nuns who publish her in France. Were rooms ever better named? The amount of "parlering" (if one can coin such a word) that goes on in them is extraordinary, and the personality of the nuns is such that the grille† seems to disappear; but to work is one thing, to succeed is another, and, as with the *Prayers from the Ark,* I am aware that I have not captured the poems in their original worth. There is an elusiveness, too, about these voices that led the poet to write the fleeting small poem at the end of this book. Yet, elusive or not, I feel Carmen de Gasztold has been able

* *The Life and Letters of Janet Erskine Stuart,* by Maud Monahan (New York: Longmans, Green, 1948).

† The nuns are enclosed.

to find for each beast its authentic voice, and this in a refreshing, matter-of-fact way; yet each large or infinitesimal, favoured or ill-favoured, bold or timid creature wafts up, as in the Prayers, an unexpected grain of incense that consecrates its wild or tame work-a-day self.

—RUMER GODDEN

Seigneur, je suis roi . . .

THE LION

ord,
I am King.
That is the law.
You know what it means
to wear a nimbus.
Some people think
they can rule by love.
How naïve!
I know how to govern
Your creatures:
strength
is all they respect.
Let us say
that fear is wholesome,
besides, I delight
in making the whole plain tremble
with one roar.
Yet, far be it from me
to do anything paltry
or low;
I know the cost of a noble heart.
That is why,
Lord,
I so love Your glory,
and strive to attain it.

Amen.

. . . je suis Votre agneau
dans ma douceur de laine.

THE LAMB

 spindle on four legs
leaving tufts of white in the thickets,
I am Your lamb,
Lord,
in my soft wool.
My bleating
sends it puny note
into the ewe's heart;
my fleece
throws its curly shadow
on the cropped grass.
Look, Lord,
how my joy must leap!
Yet my need of my mother
never sleeps in me.
Let me run to her
with my wavering steps
and draw some of her tenderness.
Oh,
don't let it happen,
Lord,
that one sad day
I will miss her.

                    Amen.

A petits pas innombrables
je traverse la vie . . .

THE CENTIPEDE

With innumerable little footsteps
I go through life
but, Lord,
I can never
get to the end of myself!
It's a queer sensation
to be a multitude
that follows itself
in Indian file!
True,
it's the first step that counts
or, rather,
the first foot.
All that matters
is to be in step
with one's self.
I only ask,
Lord,
to jog along
one in spirit
without troublesome
reticences.

Amen.

Rapide,
légère,
le coeur enlacé
de crainte sauvage . . .

THE GAZELLE

Fleet,
light,
my heart stifled
with wild fear,
always ready to leap
away with the wind,
at the least noise,
the least cry,
I bless You
Lord,
because for me
You have set no bounds
to Your space;
and if I fly,
an arrow,
on my slender legs,
my little hooves
barely skimming the ground,
it is not that I scorn
the peace of Your pools,
but so, Lord,
that my life
might be a race
run straight
to the haven of Your love.

Amen.

Moi,
je me traine, je me traine, je me traine . . .

THE SNAIL

ord,
You try for a little while
to walk on one foot
carrying Your whole heaven on Your back.
As for me,
I drag, drag, drag on,
trailed by my iridescent track,
and swaying this hollow mountain,
my small house;
but where is there a coilaway
from gardeners and hens?
You must admit, Lord,
You have made my life hard.
So many enemies!
And just to bring home
the smear of my helplessness,
these two eyes on the tips of my horns
are two timid periscopes.
Lord, You know
that someone who drags along complains.
Don't be offended
by this misanthropic heart
but, to lighten its burden,
send a paradise of lettuces—for one—
and the warmth of a thunder shower.

                    Amen.

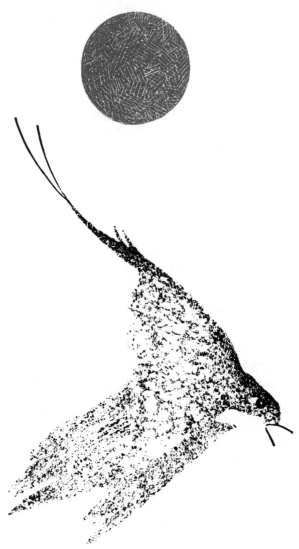

Qui vit, qui vit, qui vit,
Seigneur,
si ce n'est moi?

THE SWALLOW

Who is quick, quick, quick,
and lives, Lord,
if not I?
Small black arrow
of Your blue sky.
I stun the wind
by the swift ease
of my flight
but, under the eaves of the roof,
in their cosy clay home,
my nestlings are hungry.
Quick, quick, quick,
in the hunt for their food,
I dart
from the top to the bottom
of heaven
with a whistle of joy;
then my beak opens
to snap up some inalert fly.
Lord,
a day will come,
a chill gold day
when my babes will take wing
on their own affairs.
Oh! On that day,
when there will be nothing more to bring,
console me
with the call of countries far away.   Amen.

. . . j'ai l'air
      d'une étoile de sang.

ord,
Your deep has closed over me.
Am I
some small Lucifer
fallen from heaven
and left
to be tormented by the waves?
Look, Lord,
I seem
a star of blood.
I try to remember
my lost royalty
but in vain.
Creeping over the sand,
I spread my star-points wide
and dream, dream, dream. . . .
Lord,
an angel
could root me up
from the bottom of the sea
and set me back
in Your sky.
Oh! One day
could that be?

Amen.

Oui, Seigneur, je pique!

THE HEDGEHOG

es, Lord, I prick!
Life is not easy—
but You know that—
and I have too much on my shoulders!
I speak of my prickles
but thank You for them.
You at least
have understood me,
that is why You made me
such a pinball.
How else can I defend myself?
When people see me,
my anxious nose
searching for the fat slugs
that devastate the garden,
why can't they leave me alone?
Ah! But when I think proper,
I can roll myself up
into my hermit life.

Amen.

... la joyeuse ardeur de mes ailes
pleines de petits yeux noirs!

THE LADYBIRD

ear God,
I belong to Our Lady, Your Mother.
That isn't hard to believe;
It's written in my name.
Oh! May my midget
thanksgiving,
the small circles of my flight
across the meadow,
gladden Her heart.
How I love each blade of Your grass!
I love to land there,
resting the happy whirr of my wings—
dotted with small black eyes.
Thank You for having made me
so that no one is afraid of me:
a little toy,
a penny toy,
a mite of comfort and laughter.

Amen.

Solitaire et laid . . .

THE TOAD

Lonely and ugly—
who hasn't a horror
of me, Lord?
Yet my song trills
of an unmalicious heart.
In the night
that hides me,
I dedicate
the melancholy chant
of my unwholesomeness
to You, Lord.
Of Your mercy
graciously accept it,
and at last I shall learn
to bear my odium
with love.

Amen.

Oh! Quel souci!
Tous ces poussins . . .

THE MOTHER HEN

h! What a worrit!
All these chicks
to cherish and protect—
can't shut an eye
even for a moment!
That one strays too far,
those two big ones quarrel,
and this tiny one isn't strong.
I should like to keep them always under my wings,
but they must learn how to live.
That dreadful cat!
Never trust a cat!
And all these feet
tramping round my brood.
Beware! Hen pecks!
I'm going to lose my temper!
Lord,
my heart is so choked
with loving care,
how can I say

amen?

. . . l'orgueil a du bon
contre la soif, les mirages
et le vent de sable!

THE CAMEL

 ord,
do not be displeased.
There *is* something to be said for pride
against thirst, mirages,
and sandstorms;
and I must say
that, to face and rise above
these arid desert dramas,

two humps
are not too many,
nor an arrogant lip.
Some people criticize
my four flat feet,
the base of my pile of joints,
but what should I do
with high heels
crossing so much country,
such shifting dreams,
while upholding my dignity?
My heart wrung
by the cries of jackals and hyenas,
by the burning silence,
the magnitude of Your cold stars,
I give You thanks, Lord,
for this my realm,
wide as my longings
and the passage of my steps.
Carrying my royalty
in the aristocratic curve of my neck
from oasis to oasis,
one day shall I find again
the caravan of the magi?
And the gates of Your paradise?

Amen.

Je creuse, je creuse . . .

THE MOLE

 dig and dig,
looking
for life itself.
You have chosen darkness
for me, Lord,
and my tunnel
lengthens
in cavernous night.
Here and there,
a tiny hillock
shows above ground;
the rest
is buried
in the deep dark.
A hidden life,
Lord,
but not a poor one—
my velvet coat shows that.
In shadowy gloom
one can walk without presumption
and be perfectly safe—
but the sun
can turn one's head;
Lord, keep me from the vanities of the world,
and guide the strivings
of my little paws
so that they reach
some secret Paradise.
                    Amen.

. . . *une flèche ardente*
sur un mur de soleil.

THE LIZARD

 ord,
who has inlaid
the triangular throb
of my head
with these thirsting eyes,
and inlaid me
with a flicker quick heart,
please put me
a swift arrow
on a sun-baked wall:
a wall full of cracks,
of mossy havens,
quiet caves of shadow
and hiding places:
a wall alight with joy
and life. . . .
Let me drink at the fire of Your sky,
until a slit
in the walls of Your paradise
drinks me in, as a trickle of water
dries and is gone.

Amen.

sans doute
une plaisanterie divine . . .

THE WHALE

hat could hold me,
Lord,
except Your ocean?
My inordinate size
must obviously be
a divine joke,
but am I
perhaps
rather ridiculous,
like a blown-up blubber toy?
I am a peaceful leviathan,
on a strict diet,
a waterspout
on my nose.
My sole problem
is to choose between water and air;
but,
hunted for my mollifying oil,
I dread the whalers
who mercilessly chase me
with their iron harpoons.
I never asked
for such yards of flesh,
and where can I hide
from the lust of men?
Lord,
if only some fortunate plunge
would let me come up into
Your eternal peace.   Amen.

... *Votre soleil*
me donne
la danse de St. Guy ...

THE GNAT

 h Lord,
Your sun
gives me
St. Vitus's dance,
I,
and all my clan.
We trace our strange ballet
in the sunlight.
Yes, we, though so little,
must manifest
our joy,
and dance, dance, dance.
Oh, let our tiny black constellation
take its place, one day,
glorified
as stars.

Amen.

Je suis
quelque peu bavard . . .

 ## THE PARROT

id you say something,
Lord?
Oh! I thought
You were speaking to me.
You are silent?
Are You afraid
I shall tell

Your secrets?
It's true
I'm a little talkative
but, at times,
that is useful:
heads are thick,
slow to understand,
and have to be told things
again and again.
If You need me,
I am Your servant,
one who never grows tired
repeating the same word
again and again,
which has its power:
I may grow tedious
but people listen
in spite of themselves;
and what is repeated,
repeated, repeated,
stays in the memory.
When may I serve
Your infinite wisdom?
Think of it, Lord.

Amen.

. . . au centre
de mon grand filet
de soie,
fragile et fort . . .

THE SPIDER

I thank You,
dear God,
for the arches
of my long legs—
a spinner's legs.
In the middle
of my wide silken net,
fragile and strong
in the shifting wind,
I wait for my meat and drink
and thank You,
dear God.
Between branches in the garden
I fish for frost and dew.
In the corners of dead rooms,
in dark attics,
I fish for sombreness,
lonely relinquishment,
and I thank You,
dear God.
In the nimble silence
of my life,
on the thread of my airy dreams,
in the geometric tracery of my thoughts,
I thank You,
forever, dear God.

Amen.

Vous m'avez faite
tenace à ce qui m'attire. . . .

THE FLY

ord,
shall I always go in black
for this life?
Fugitive from its tumult
on my transparent wings,
humming my prayers
and pausing weightless
on my thin legs,
I,
whom the world finds such a burden?
You have made me
stick to what lures me.
Yet, if I am caught
clinging there,
don't let me die
like the poor useless
thing that I am.

Amen.

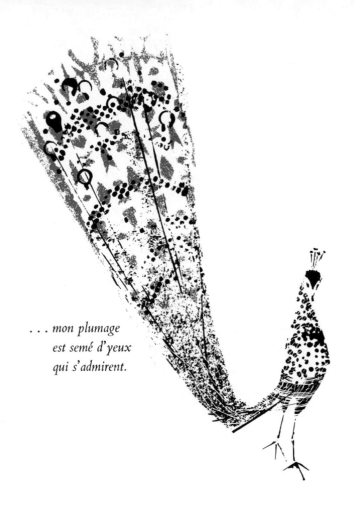

*. . . mon plumage
est semé d'yeux
qui s'admirent.*

THE PEACOCK

 royal train,
Lord,
more scintillating
than jewelled enamel.

Look,
now I spread it in a wheel.
I must say I derive
some satisfaction
from my good looks.
My feathers
are sown with eyes
admiring themselves.
True,
my discordant cry
shames me a little—
and it is humiliating
to make me remember
my meagre heart.
Your world is badly made,
if I may say so:
the nightingale's voice
in me
would be properly attired—
and soothe my soul.
Lord,
let a day come,
a heavenly day,
when my inner and outer selves
will be reconciled
in perfect harmony.

                    Amen.

Humide et glauque
dans ma petite maison
de nacre . . .

THE OYSTER

Moist, glaucous,
in my mother-of-pearl house,
its door tightly shut
against intruders,
I drink in a dream from the sea:
Oh, let an iridescent pearl—
a milky dawn,
a faerie sheen—
find its tints in the heart of my life.
Then if, slowly,
day by day,
this mysterious seed
grows more perfect,
for my joy
and Your glory,
Lord,
nothing else will matter.
If it must be, I shall die
to let it reach its fullest splendour,
shining—only for You,
Lord—
at the bottom of the sea.

Amen.

Je suis l'oiseau
de l'amertume sans fond,
blanc et gris
comme le sel. . . .

THE SEAGULL

A hole in the cliffs
is my nest but the sea calls me,
and I cradle my dreams
in the hollows of the waves.
The roll of Your ocean
is with me in the sky,
where I swing
on one wing, then the other,
and plummet
like a stone
on the living flash
of a fish.
Lord,
does my poignant cry
echo the endless travail
that beats on Your shore?
I am the bird
like salt,
grey and white,
a bitter tang
that does not fade;
and the ships
outward bound
watch me out of sight,
a little handkerchief
waving goodbye.
In the restlessness of my kingdom,
Lord,
let the storm spare me.   Amen.

Seigneur,
ayez pitié
de mon coeur d'ours.

THE BEAR

To have my name
among the stars,
then to think
I may end as a bedside rug!
Oh, Lord,
this thought makes me
terribly gruff.
Large-pawed, clumsy—
no teddy bear—
I am more shrewd
than people think,
and I know
all about climbing trees!
If I could find
a honeycomb,
my carnivorous soul
would not scorn its sweetness.
Sweetness!
There are men
who tame me,
and make me dance
to their piping;
or put me in a cage,
I, who was born to be free
like all self-respecting beasts.
Lord, have pity
on my bearish heart.
See to it
I meet no hunters.   Amen.

Je saute, je pique,
je saute, je pique!

THE FLEA

I jump.   I bite.
I jump.   I bite.
How it amuses me,
Lord!
How ingenious
to have made me so small,
with this springboard leap!
I jump.   I bite.
I jump.   I bite.
A royal game.
I own I put
a spice of malice in it,
and I have more power
to upset the world
than the elephant.
When I think of that
I could die of laughing.
I jump.   I bite.
I jump.   I bite.
Lord,
will You let me
into Your paradise
and not be afraid
that I shall turn it upside down?
I dare not say

                    amen.

. . . je ne demande
qu'à bâtir
Votre paradis.

THE BEAVER

o build,
Lord,
that is a vocation!
I speak of my passion,
architecture.
Of course
one should build on a rock,
but what fillip is there
in doing anything easy?

My element
is to struggle—
it is water that allures—
and tell me
to build a safe and steady house
on the moving stream
of a river—
moving as life does, swiftly—
what an adventure!
With patience and ingenuity
one can do anything.
But I am one
who loves to swim against the current,
to build
something lasting—
and all my own work—
at the very core of life.
Oh yes, Lord,
if You would give me
some of Your living water,
I would build
Your paradise for You.

Amen.

Little song,
where is your heart?
In passing
you throw me a quick word
and escape on the wind.
I wish I could catch you
by the tip of a wing,
to get to know you,
laugh and cry with you.
Little song,
nobody's, anybody's,
you take your own fanciful way,
and drop your words
one by one
into my ear
and are gone.
Little song,
where is your heart?

W HEN CARMEN BERNOS DE GASZTOLD was a child in her mother's tall house in Arcachon, she used to run down the flights of stairs so quickly that she really believed she was flying, a fitting belief for the poet who was one day to write "The Lark."

Arachon is in France, in the province of Bordeaux, a small town set between pine forests and the sea. On the father's side, the great-grandfather was Lithuanian, and this Slavonic blood seems to have mingled in his family the paradox of its dark melancholy and sparkling vivacity with the steady reserve of the provincial French. It was an unusual family, and, as Carmen Bernos says, not practical: Monsieur de Gasztold was professor of Spanish at Arcachon, but the household was overshadowed by his inability to make enough money to keep his growing family. Scheme after scheme was tried; he bought a machine for pleating cloth; then a button machine,★ but one after another the schemes failed. He was, too, often seriously ill, and then the younger children were sent away for the day to the Sisters of Saint Joseph, and for Carmen there began the terror and horror she always met when away from home. What to more ordinary people is simply sad, humdrum, or hard, to a poet can be excruciating. Carmen's

★ This gives me a fellow feeling with the poet. My father, too, bought a button machine, to make pearl buttons from the mother-of-pearl linings of the mussel shells that abound in the Brahmaputra River of Bengal. It might have made money, only no one ever found out how to separate the pearl from the shell.

first memories are of two cots, one red, one white; her sister Micheline in the white, uninhibitedly turning somersaults, while she herself crouched in the red one, peering through the bars, too afraid of doing something wrong to move. Trivial things happened that to her were searing. She saw a mistress put a donkey's head on a stupid child in class; worse, a nun once said to her kindly, "Now you are my little girl." "I am Maman's, Maman's," she had sobbed, terribly distressed. Still, there were compensations in being Carmen; Micheline had difficulty in learning to read; the younger Carmen, standing beside the teacher's knees, read the book—upside down.

There were five children, close as only children surrounded by an unsympathetic world can be. To the good people of Bordeaux, money was the measure of position, and these children, whom one can guess to have been beautifully mannered, delicate in thought and feeling, often suffered acutely from their father's lack of success. "Play by yourselves," their mother told them, and they grew up in a proud family solitude.

The eldest girl, Simone, succeeded in getting a post as a teacher in the Collège Sainte Marie at Neuilly near Paris, run by the famous Madame Daniélou under the guidance of the Jesuits. When Carmen was twelve, Simone persuaded Madame to take her small sister on a bursary, and for the rest of Carmen's school life the Collège provided everything; but she found the life of a boarding school terribly shut in; she could not sleep and was plagued by a bad memory which made it difficult for her to learn. In the end she gave up trying to get her diploma and felt she had failed Madame Daniélou. Yet it was the Révérend Père Daniélou who, some years later, published Carmen's first poems in the magazine *Études*.

Meanwhile at home things had grown steadily worse. Her father was in hospital and no longer knew his family, a great grief to Carmen, who did not understand he had gone out of his mind but thought that he had ceased to love them. If the house had not been Madame de Gasztold's, it would have been sold. At last Monsieur de Gasztold died. Childhood was over. At sixteen Carmen had to leave Neuilly and start to earn her living.

She began teaching children but was so shy that she walked round and round the pupils' houses, not daring to go in.

When war broke out she was a governess in Normandy but had fortunately come home to Arcachon for the baptism of the first of Simone's eight children. For a while she stayed on with her mother at Arcachon, but, having no means of living there, they were forced to go back to Neuilly, where they had a small apartment. They had to sell the mother's remaining jewelry to get there, and give up the house.

For seven years Carmen Bernos worked in a laboratory of an artificial silk factory, helping to support her mother and, in the years before the war ended, enduring all the hardship, lack of proper food and fuel, the restrictions, petty and big, of the German occupation, as well as the harassing days at the laboratory. Yet it was in this time that, one evening, as Carmen was writing to a friend, a poem suddenly came. "It was there—on the page," says Carmen. After that she wrote secretly, at every free moment, huddled in an old eiderdown to keep herself warm, choosing her ice-cold room rather than the one in which the family gathered around the one stove of the apartment. The poems poured out— all the poems of *Le Mieux Aimè*.

The war was over, but that brought no ease. In 1945 the mother died, and with her death the whole world seemed to fall to pieces. The Arcachon home was gone. Carmen had given up her work at the laboratory and was a governess once more in a French family at Lisbon. There a friend of the family, a Russian by birth, fell in love with the bewildered, homesick girl who was also extremely beautiful. Carmen Bernos is beautiful. Her head is as proudly set as the young Napoleon's in the painting; she is dark, with fine bones, and her brown eyes are so eloquent she hardly needs to talk. On the eve of the marriage Carmen, uncertain about her own feelings, broke the engagement. Then at last she found work she loved, teaching the kindergarten class of Sainte Marie every afternoon—she had thirty children to look after—but in an effort to help Micheline, who was in difficulties, she accepted the charge of teaching another class in the morning. For the delicate, highly wrought girl the strain was too much, and there was a breakdown, physical and mental, serious.

It seemed that there was no one to help at the moment of this illness, the brothers and sisters had troubles of their own, but a lifelong friend of the family's was a nun in the enclosed order of Saint Benedict, and now the Mother Abbess of the Community sent for Carmen and took her under her wing. Their well-known monastery in the Rue Monsieur in Paris had had to be given up, and they were now building the new Abbaye of Saint Louis du Temple at Limon-par-Igny, just south of Paris. Standing in a great park, the Abbaye, with its yellow stone walls, cloisters, great chapter house, fine staircase, guest parlours, and chapel, plain yet noble with its marble floors, stone vaulted ceiling, and exquisite modern stained glass, has been built by the community, using mainly workmen nobody else would employ. For more than four years the nuns nursed Carmen, keeping her on their farm and encouraging her to write; besides *Prayers from the Ark* and *The Creatures' Choir*, she has written other poems and several books for children. Everyone worked; indeed, the Abbaye might be the hive in "The Prayer of the Bee":

> *Que ma petite parcelle d'ardente vie*
> *se fonde dans la grande activité communautaire*
> *pour que s'élève, à votre gloire,*
> *ce temple de douceur,*
> *cette citadelle d'encens,*
> *ce grand cierge cloisonné*
> *pétri de vos grâces*
> *et de mon obscur labeur!*
>
> > *Amen*

A good atmosphere in which to get well, and Carmen Bernos was cured, but now, though she goes away to stay with her brothers and sisters, the Abbaye has become home and she lives and works "*dans l'ombre de l'Abbaye,*" as she puts it and is their cherished "child." Her room is in the Tower, the great old *colombier*, or dove house, recently made into an extra guest house; it is here that she writes, working meanwhile in the Abbaye library and as a fitter on the stained-glass windows with their jewel-bright colours.